D1117071

DEC - - 2000

Seven Natural Wonders
of the
ARCTIC, ANTARCTICA, and the OCEANS

Michael Woods and Mary B. Woods

TWENTY-FIRST CENTURY BOOKS

Minneapolis

To Jane Shure

Copyright © 2009 by Michael Woods and Mary B. Woods

All rights reserved. International copyright secured. No part of this book may be reproduced, stored in a retrieval system, or transmitted in any form or by any means—electronic, mechanical, photocopying, recording, or otherwise—without the prior written permission of Lerner Publishing Group, Inc., except for the inclusion of brief quotations in an acknowledged review.

Twenty-First Century Books
A division of Lerner Publishing Group, Inc.
241 First Avenue North
Minneapolis, MN 55401 U.S.A.

Website address: www.lernerbooks.com

Library of Congress Cataloging-in-Publication Data

Woods, Michael, 1946–
      Seven natural wonders of the Arctic, Antarctica, and the Oceans / by Michael Woods and Mary B. Woods.
         p.   cm. — (Seven wonders)
      Includes bibliographical references and index.
      ISBN 978–0–8225–9075–0 (lib. bdg. : alk. paper)
      1. Natural history—Polar regions—Juvenile literature. 2. Landforms—Polar regions—Juvenile literature.
   3. Ocean—Juvenile literature. I. Woods, Mary B. (Mary Boyle), 1946– II. Title.
   QH84.1.W68 2009
   508.3162—dc22   2008025270

Manufactured in the United States of America
1 2 3 4 5 6 – DP – 14 13 12 11 10 09

Contents

INTRODUCTION

*P*EOPLE LOVE TO MAKE LISTS OF THE BIGGEST AND THE BEST. ALMOST TWENTY-FIVE HUNDRED YEARS AGO, A GREEK WRITER NAMED HERODOTUS MADE A LIST OF THE MOST AWESOME THINGS EVER BUILT BY PEOPLE. THE LIST INCLUDED BUILDINGS, STATUES, AND OTHER OBJECTS THAT WERE LARGE, WONDROUS, AND IMPRESSIVE. LATER, OTHER WRITERS ADDED NEW ITEMS TO THE LIST. WRITERS EVENTUALLY AGREED ON A FINAL LIST. IT WAS CALLED THE SEVEN WONDERS OF THE ANCIENT WORLD.

The list became so famous that people began imitating it. They made other lists of wonders. They listed Seven Wonders of the Modern World and Seven Wonders of the Middle Ages. People even made lists of undersea wonders.

People also made lists of natural wonders. Natural wonders are extraordinary things created by nature, without help from people. Earth is full of natural wonders, so it has been hard for people to choose the absolute best. Over the years, different people have made different lists of the Seven Wonders of the Natural World.

This book explores seven wonders of the oceans and the polar regions—the Arctic and Antarctica. Like Earth as a whole, these areas have far more than seven natural wonders. But even if people can never agree on which ones are the greatest, these seven choices are sure to amaze you.

WONDERFUL WATER

Ocean water covers about 71 percent of Earth's surface. Mapmakers divide this huge body of salt water into five oceans: the Atlantic, Pacific, Indian, Arctic, and Antarctic (sometimes called the Southern Ocean). The deep oceans are some of the last unexplored places on Earth. In fact, more people have walked on the moon than have been to the deepest parts of the ocean.

The Arctic and Antarctica also have had few visitors. The Arctic ice cap is a layer of ice that floats on the Arctic Ocean, covering the northernmost part of Earth. The ice cap shrinks each summer as ice melts. It grows again in the winter as water freezes. The continent of Antarctica, in contrast, is a landmass. But you may never see its land. It lies under a thick sheet of ice and snow at Earth's southern end. What the Arctic and Antarctica have in common are the harshest environments on the planet. They are remote, bitterly cold, windswept places.

WONDERFUL ADVENTURE

This book will take you on a tour of natural wonders of the oceans, the Arctic, and Antarctica. One stop will be the deepest abyss of the ocean, the Mariana Trench. There, glowing sea creatures use their light to attract prey in the extremely dark and cold environment. The tour will also visit tropical ocean waters and the Great Barrier Reef. This chain of coral reefs is home to the most diverse sea life on Earth. Another stop will be the Bay of Fundy in Canada. Twice each day, the water level rises as much as 50 feet (15 meters). It could cover a five-story building. You'll also venture to Antarctica. That continent is so different from the rest of Earth that NASA (the National Aeronautics and Space Administration) uses it to test spacecraft headed for Mars. Read on to explore other wonders, from the ends of the Earth to the depths of the oceans.

Colorful sea lilies grow on the Great Barrier Reef.

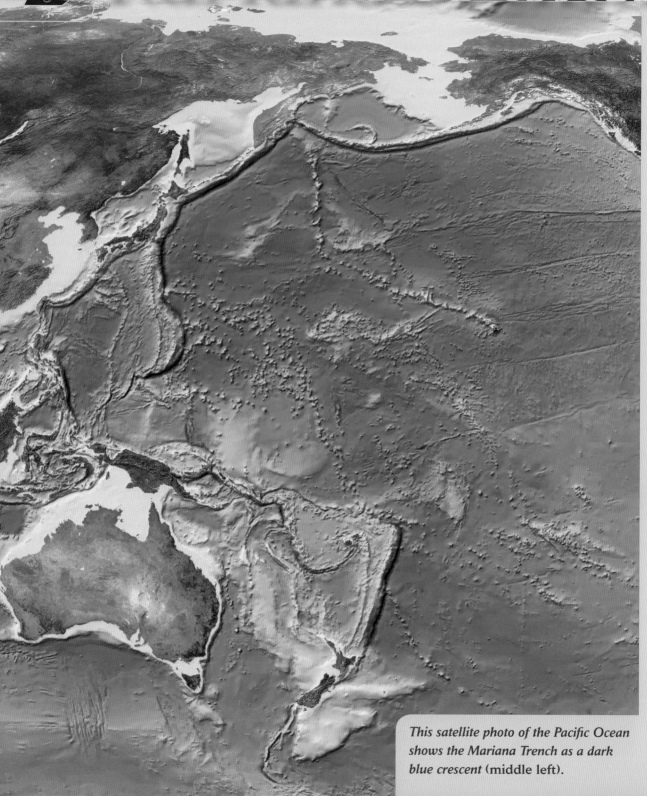

This satellite photo of the Pacific Ocean shows the Mariana Trench as a dark blue crescent (middle left).

$\mathcal{M}$ANY PEOPLE KNOW THAT THE HIGHEST POINT ON EARTH IS AT THE TOP OF MOUNT EVEREST. THAT FAMOUS PEAK TOWERS 29,035 FEET (8,850 M) ABOVE SEA LEVEL. IT IS IN THE HIMALAYA MOUNTAINS, NEAR THE BORDER OF CHINA AND NEPAL. BUT HOW MANY PEOPLE CAN NAME THE LOWEST PLACE IN THE WORLD? THAT POINT IS AT THE BOTTOM OF THE MARIANA TRENCH, A VALLEY IN THE FLOOR OF THE PACIFIC OCEAN. THE TRENCH LIES JUST EAST OF THE MARIANA ISLANDS, SOUTHEAST OF CHINA AND JAPAN.

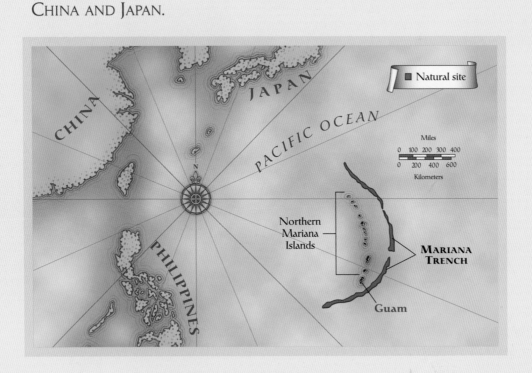

Above: *Mount Everest, the highest point on Earth, lies on the border between Nepal and Tibet.* Inset: *In this satellite image, the deepest areas of the Mariana Trench appear in dark blue.*

This enormous trench extends for about 1,554 miles (2,500 kilometers) from one end to the other. It could stretch from New York City almost to Denver, Colorado. The trench averages about 45 miles (72 km) wide. A person walking at a brisk pace would need about ten hours to go from one side to the other.

Inside that groove in the ocean floor is the Challenger Deep, the deepest spot in the world. It lies 210 miles (338 km) from the island of Guam. It is about 36,000 feet (11,000 m) below sea level—almost 7 miles (11 km) deep. If Mount Everest were placed in the Challenger Deep, the mountain's peak would still be under 7,000 feet (2,134 m) of water.

EVER *Wonder?*

Why is it pitch dark in the deep ocean? In the oceans, deeper means dimmer. Water absorbs and scatters sunlight. So, little light remains after 660 feet (201 m). Beyond that depth is a twilight zone, where the human eye cannot see colors. This zone of faint light goes down to about 3,300 feet (1,006 m). The midnight zone, from there on down, is in total darkness.

WEIRD CREATURES

Conditions are very harsh at the summit of Mount Everest. Temperatures average −33°F (−36°C), and winter winds howl at more than 100 miles (161 km) an hour. Yet climbers have reached the top and lived to tell about it.

But no human, not even an expert diver, could survive the environment of the Challenger Deep. In this pitch-black world, the temperature is about 36°F (2°C). The human body shuts down quickly in water that cold. A person on the ocean floor also would be crushed by the weight of the water. Water is heavy. A 1-gallon (4-liter) milk jug holds about 8 pounds (3.6 kilograms) of water. At the deepest point in the ocean, water would press down with a weight heavier than hundreds of elephants.

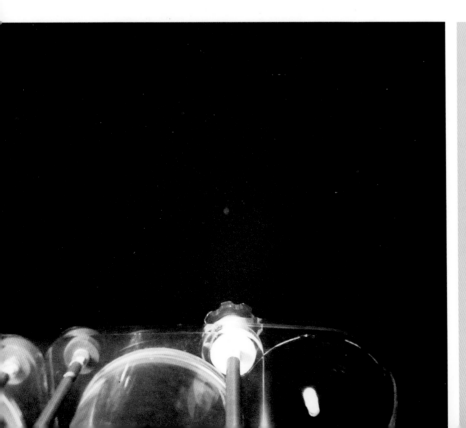

A research vessel shines a light into the Challenger Deep. No natural light reaches the extreme depths of the Mariana Trench.

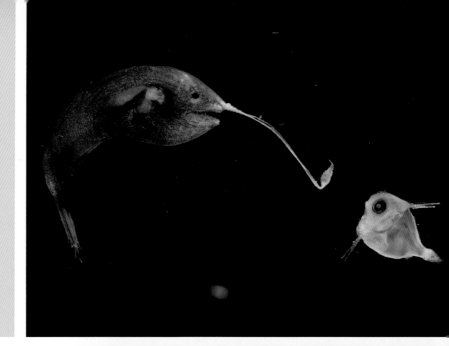

Right: *An anglerfish uses its natural fishing pole to lure prey into its mouth.*
Below: *Flashlight fish have glowing patches just beneath their eyes.*

However, living things do thrive in the Mariana Trench. Some creatures look like deep-sea movie monsters or survivors from prehistoric times. These animals and plants are specially built for life in an extreme environment. Some can produce a glowing light, like fireflies. This is called bioluminescence. Creatures use this light to attract prey.

Anglerfish have bioluminescent, built-in fishing poles. In some of these fish, the pole is like an antenna growing from the top of the head. This rod glows in the dark water. The anglerfish waves it to attract other fish. When a fish approaches, the angler snaps up the prey in its huge mouth packed with long, needle-sharp teeth.

Flashlight fish also live in the Mariana Trench. Like the anglerfish, they are bioluminescent. The flashlight fish lurks in the dark water and turns its light on and off. When a curious fish approaches, it becomes dinner!

"A world as strange as that of Mars."
—*William Beebe, an explorer, describing the deep ocean after setting a world record in 1934 by diving to 3,028 feet (923 m) in a submersible (small submarine)*

Below top: *A deep-water photograph exposes crabs, anemones, and snails on the floor of the Mariana Trench.*
Below bottom: *A dredging boat from the HMS* Challenger *prepares to collect samples from the ocean floor.*

Certain types of crabs and bacteria thrive in the Mariana Trench. Scientists had never seen some of these until fairly recent deep-sea explorations. This is because the creatures can't exist anywhere else. The extreme temperatures and pressure of the deep ocean are vital to these organisms.

CHALLENGER LOOKS DEEP

The Mariana Trench was discovered in 1875. Scientists on the British ship HMS *Challenger* used a machine to measure the ocean depth in different places. The machine unreeled a spool of wire with a heavy weight at the end. Dials measured the length of wire let out. When the weight touched bottom, scientists could tell the depth of the ocean floor. With that simple method, they realized that the water near the Mariana Islands was extremely deep.

In 1951 the British Royal Navy vessel HMS *Challenger II* returned to the area with a modern measuring device. It is called echo sounding, or sonar. It sends out sound waves that bounce off a surface, such as the seafloor. Scientists measured the time needed for sound waves to bounce back from the seafloor to the ship. This told them the ocean depth. Using echo sounding, *Challenger II* mapped the entire Mariana Trench. The deepest point it found was 35,760 feet (10,900 m). That point was named the Challenger Deep, after the ship.

People got their first glimpse of the Challenger Deep in 1960. That year scientist Jacques Piccard and U.S. Navy lieutenant Don Walsh traveled to the bottom. They rode in the *Trieste*, a submersible vehicle. Small submarines of this kind are built to withstand extreme underwater pressure. They usually carry scientific instruments for exploring the deep ocean. Piccard and Walsh found a point deeper than *Challenger II* had found. It was 35,813 feet (10,916 m) below the surface. They also observed small fish near the ocean floor.

Since then oceanographers have used other vehicles and instruments to explore the deep ocean. Some are remotely operated vehicles, or ROVs. Scientists control these through cables from a ship on the

THE MOON over *Mariana*

Twelve U.S. astronauts have been on the moon. They explored the moon's surface in the 1960s and 1970s during the Apollo space program. However, only two people have ever visited the deepest place on Earth. Don Walsh *(below left)* and Jacques Piccard *(below right)* spent just twenty minutes there during their descent in the *Trieste* submersible in 1960.

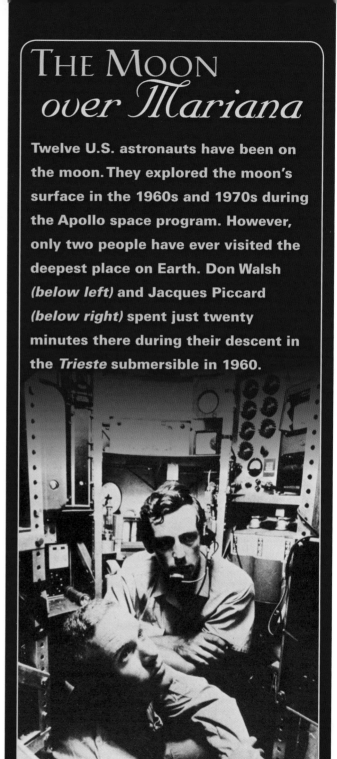

"A pretty hairy experience."
—U.S. Navy lieutenant Don Walsh, after a window on the Trieste cracked during its famous dive into the Challenger Deep in 1960

surface. Others are autonomous underwater vehicles, or AUVs. These explore on their own without any connection to another ship. AUVs navigate with onboard computers and record data from the areas they explore.

In the 1990s, several Japanese ROVs explored the Mariana Trench. They observed shrimp, sandworms, and other living things. The ROV *Kaiko* scooped up samples of mud from the trench floor for scientists to study. Scientists found tiny organisms in those samples that are Earth's deepest living creatures.

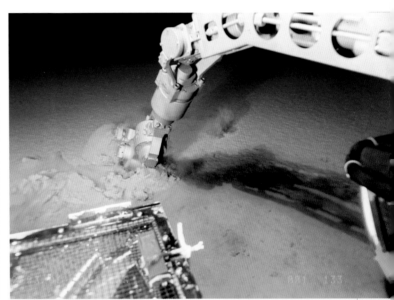

Right: *Japanese scientists direct* Kaiko *to retrieve soil samples from the bottom of the Mariana Trench using a robotic arm.* **Below left:** *The ROV* Hercules, *operated by researchers from the United States, was designed to operate in extremely deep water.* **Below right:** *A crane holds the ROV* Kaiko *just before launch.*

PLATES SO DEEP

The Mariana Trench is so deep because of movement in Earth's surface. Many huge plates of rock make up the surface. Earth's crust, or outer layer, forms the top of each plate. The bottom of each plate is part of Earth's mantle, the thick layer below the crust. The plates float on a layer of puttylike rock in the mantle. While floating, the edges of these plates slide past one another and bump into one another.

At the Mariana Trench, a heavy plate of rock on the ocean floor is pressing against a plate of lighter rock. When this happens, the heavier ocean plate plunges downward at a steep angle into Earth's mantle. The bottom of the Mariana Trench is where that heavy plate of rock is moving down into the mantle.

Plate movements have formed more than twenty other deep ocean trenches in different parts of the world. The Puerto Rico Trench, for instance, is the deepest place in the Atlantic Ocean. It lies north of the island of Puerto Rico. The trench is about 5 miles (8 km) deep and 1,100 miles (1,770 km) long.

At the Mariana Trench, the movement of ocean plates into Earth's mantle created many underwater volcanoes. This cliff near the Mariana Trench shows layers of light and dark ash that collected on the seafloor during eruptions.

The Mariana Trench is not threatened by humans. But the Mariana Islands on its edge are home to many endangered species of fish and marine plants. People in the Northern Mariana Islands hope to make Asuncion Island (above) *and several nearby islands into a national monument protected from overfishing and pollution.*

MARIANA TRENCH *Expressway*

Navy submarines patrolling the world's oceans like to stay in deep water. Military submarines are safer in deep water. It is more difficult for enemies to detect them there. That's why U.S., Russian, and other submarines often use the Mariana Trench as an expressway. The trench is the main north-south route for submarines in the Pacific Ocean.

WORRIES ABOUT THE WONDER

The future of the Mariana Trench seems very safe. Neither people nor nature threatens its existence. Ships sailing over the area do not cause any damage to the trench. However, movements of Earth's plates may eventually change the Mariana Trench. In millions of years, it may be deeper or shallower. But it is sure to remain a wonder that holds many secrets of the deep.

THE
Gulf Stream

The warm waters of the Gulf Stream flow in an easterly direction, starting off the coast of Florida (above).

*I*N THE 1700S, THE JOURNEY FROM ENGLAND TO THE AMERICAN COLONIES TOOK ABOUT TWO MONTHS ABOARD A SHIP. THE LONG VOYAGE WAS THE ONLY WAY TO GET PEOPLE AND SUPPLIES ACROSS THE ATLANTIC OCEAN. BENJAMIN FRANKLIN NOTICED THAT SHIPS CARRYING MAIL FROM GREAT BRITAIN TO THE COLONIES TOOK LONGER THAN OTHER SHIPS GOING THAT WAY— WEEKS LONGER. HE WONDERED WHY TRAVELING THE SAME DISTANCE TOOK SO MUCH MORE TIME.

Franklin's cousin Timothy Folger was a sailor. He helped Franklin find the answer. The delays were caused by the Gulf Stream—an enormous "river" of water flowing across the Atlantic.

"Although they had great wind [in the ship's sails], they could not proceed forward, but backward. . . . [Finally they realized] that the current was more powerful than the wind."

—Antonio de Herrera y Tordesillas's retelling of Spanish explorer Juan Ponce de León's 1513 voyage to the Americas

Starting in the Gulf of Mexico, water travels around the southern tip of Florida. It then flows north along the east coast of North America and east toward Europe. Mail ships from Great Britain were going against the flow. That slowed them down. Other ships traveling west seemed to know how to avoid getting caught in the eastward flow. Ships going east from the colonies to Europe, in contrast, got a free ride in the swiftly flowing water.

This satellite image of the southeastern coast of the United States shows the warm waters of the Gulf Stream in green and light blue. Cooler waters appear in dark blue and purple. In some areas, warm water separates from the Gulf Stream and drifts away, creating temporary warm spots in the ocean.

Benjamin Franklin drew this map of the Gulf Stream in the late 1700s.

In 1762 Franklin named this mighty river in the ocean the Gulf Stream. Sailors had known about it since the 1500s. Franklin used ships' records from those days to make the first map of the Gulf Stream.

The Gulf Stream is one of Earth's major ocean currents. Unlike waves and tides, you can't see currents from the coast. But these streams carry large amounts of water from one part of the ocean to another.

Currents do more than just slow down or speed up ships. They affect climates around the world. For example, compare the Labrador Coast of Canada with Cornwall in southwestern England. These regions are on the same latitude, meaning that they are the same distance from the equator. So you might think they would have similar weather.

That's not the case. Labrador has an almost arctic climate. Its daytime temperatures in January average 9°F (−12°C). But palm trees grow in Cornwall, and temperatures there rarely dip below freezing. The Gulf Stream helps to explain the different climates. It carries warm, tropical water

"This [Gulf] Stream is probably generated by the accumulation of water on the eastern coast of America between the tropics, by the trade winds that constantly blow there."

—Benjamin Franklin, writing about the Gulf Stream in about 1770

The Gulf Stream warms the waters around the town of Saint Ives, Cornwall, in England. Saint Ives is home to tropical gardens and sunny beaches. It is popular with surfers from around the world.

from the Gulf of Mexico to the coast of northwestern Europe. This water brings humid, mild air with it. That keeps temperatures in these areas much warmer than in Canada.

RIVERS IN THE OCEAN

More water flows through ocean currents than in all the world's rivers combined. The Gulf Stream alone carries more water than the Mississippi River, the Nile and the Congo in Africa, the

FEEL THAT *Current*

If you've been at an ocean beach in the summer, you may have felt ocean currents without realizing it. Standing in chest-deep water, you got goose bumps as cold water flowed around your feet and knees. From your knees to your chest, the water was warm. You were feeling warm surface currents and cold deep currents.

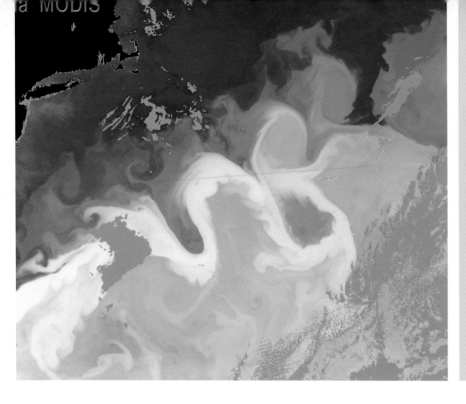

In this satellite image, the warmest waters of the Gulf Stream appear in pink. The current is leaving the coast of the United States and flowing deeper into the Atlantic Ocean.

Amazon in South America, the Volga in Russia, and the Yangtze in China. The Gulf Stream is 50 to 93 miles (80 to 150 km) wide and 2,625 to 3,937 feet (800 to 1,200 m) deep. It flows at 4.5 miles (7.2 km) per hour.

In addition to the Gulf Stream, Earth has more than twenty major ocean currents. Currents flow through all the oceans. Some currents, including the Gulf Stream, are surface currents that flow near the top of the water. Wind blowing over the surface helps to create these currents. Wind pushes the water, like ripples on the surface of a pond. It sets water in motion down to a depth of about 325 feet (100 m). Earth's rotation also affects currents. This is called the Coriolis force. The rotation causes water to move to the right in the Northern Hemisphere and to the left in the Southern Hemisphere.

"There is a river in the ocean. In the severest droughts it never fails, and in the mightiest floods it never overflows. . . . It is the Gulf Stream. There is in the world no other such majestic flow of waters. Its current is more rapid than the Mississippi or the Amazon."
—U.S. oceanographer Matthew Maury, writing in 1855

GLOBAL CONVEYOR BELT

At first, oceanographers thought that currents existed only on the surface. They knew that winds do not move deep ocean water. But scientists realized later that oceans also have deep currents. Changes in the density, or heaviness, of seawater cause these currents.

Surface water can become ice when it meets freezing air. As it freezes, the seawater leaves behind much of its salt. A layer of very salty water collects on the surface of the ocean. The salt makes this surface water heavier, so it sinks. The sinking pushes the surrounding water out of the way. That movement creates deep currents.

This process takes place in several cold regions of the oceans, including the Greenland, Labrador, and Norwegian seas in the Northern Hemisphere. From there, water flows south and west. In the Southern Hemisphere, water from the Weddell and Ross seas travels east and north past Antarctica.

Scientists call this flow of water thermohaline circulation. (*Thermo-* means "heat," and *haline* means "salt.") The Gulf Stream is part of thermohaline circulation. Warm water in the Gulf Stream evaporates as it moves north. Evaporation leaves cooler water behind. It also leaves salt, as when sea ice forms. That makes cool, dense water that sinks.

Thermohaline circulation links Earth's oceans in a chain of currents. Oceanographers call this the global conveyor belt. The main driving force for the global conveyor belt is North Atlantic Ocean water. That cold, dense, salty water sinks and flows south. But sea ice forming around

An iceberg floats near the Labrador coast of eastern Canada. Icebergs break off the huge glaciers of the northern Atlantic Ocean and float into the Gulf Stream, where they melt.

How did scientists first trace the paths of ocean currents? Some of that information came from studying charts or maps made by sailors. Scientists got more information from drift bottles. Over time, scientists have dropped many bottles containing slips of paper into currents. The paper gives the location where the bottle was released and the scientist's name and address. It includes a request to anyone who recovers it: Please tell me where you found this bottle. By tracing the paths of enough drift bottles, scientists were able to make maps of currents.

Antarctica also leaves cold, salty water. This water sinks and pushes water north again. It gradually warms and rises to the surface in the Pacific and Indian oceans.

WORRIES ABOUT THE WONDER

In the past, only sailors and oceanographers were interested in ocean currents. But currents have become a worldwide concern because of global warming. Global warming is the recent warming of Earth's surface due to more heat-trapping gases in the air. Scientists are concerned that this change in Earth's climate could affect thermohaline circulation.

It could happen in a simple way. If the climate warmed enough, the formation of sea ice may decrease or even stop. That would cut off the source of cold, salty, dense water that drives the ocean conveyor belt.

Nobody knows for certain what the consequences would be. One result might be that winter temperatures in Europe would plunge. Scientists think that such a change could happen fairly quickly. If the ocean conveyor belt shut down, winter temperatures in the North Atlantic region could fall by 20°F (11°C) or more within ten years. Parts of the United Kingdom and Ireland could wind up with an arctic climate.

3 Hydrothermal Vents

Cloudy water billows out of a vent on the floor of the Atlantic Ocean.

SCIENTISTS WERE EXPLORING A STRANGE NEW WORLD IN 1977. THEY WERE DEEP IN THE PACIFIC OCEAN, IN THE SUBMERSIBLE VEHICLE *ALVIN*. A SHIP ON THE SURFACE HAD LOWERED THE SMALL SUBMARINE INTO THE WATER ABOUT 500 MILES (805 KM) WEST OF ECUADOR, SOUTH AMERICA, NEAR THE GALÁPAGOS ISLANDS. THE ENVIRONMENT OUTSIDE *ALVIN* WAS AS UNFAMILIAR AS OUTER SPACE.

The three scientists aboard *Alvin* had traveled down for almost ninety minutes, to about 8,500 feet (2,591 m) below the surface. No sunlight reached that depth. The water looked pitch black. And the pressure was 250 times greater than on the surface.

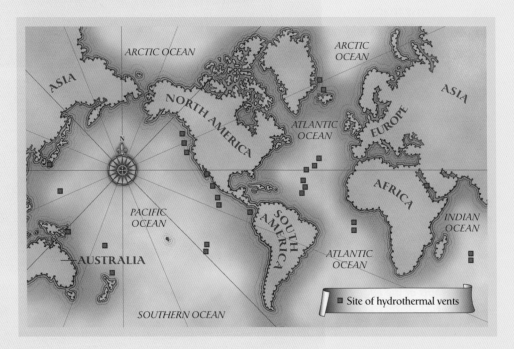

Site of hydrothermal vents

Microbes provide food for deep-sea animals in two ways. Some are eaten by snails or shrimp, which in turn become food for crabs and fish. Other microbes live inside the bodies of other animals. The microbes release nutrients that provide some of the animals' food.

CREATURES WITH WEIRD FEATURES

Scientists were shocked by the creatures the *Alvin* discovered. They had never seen most of them before. Giant red clams as big as footballs, white crabs with no eyes, and a purple octopus were just a few of the animals they found. The crew had expected to use *Alvin*'s mechanical arms only to pick up samples of rock. But they happily collected samples of these unique life-forms to study more closely.

Over the next few days, *Alvin* took other trips into the deep. It discovered more oases on the ocean floor. Scientists named one area the Dandelion Patch. It was covered with huge wormlike creatures that looked like dandelions. Stemlike bodies

Godzilla: MONSTER ON THE SEAFLOOR

Some undersea chimneys look so impressive that scientists name them after science-fiction monsters. In 1991 oceanographers discovered a monstrous black smoker chimney off the coast of Washington State. It was as high as a fifteen-story building and 40 feet (12 m) wide. An enormous black cloud of smoky water billowed from its top. Scientists named it Godzilla (below). Other gigantic chimneys have been named Sasquatch, Mothra, and the Hulk.

"When it became my turn to dive again . . . I was overwhelmed. Never before or since have I seen so much strange and exotic life."

—*Robert Ballard, an oceanographer, describing creatures he saw during a 1979 expedition aboard* Alvin

Tubeworms grow near hydrothermal vents. They can reach up to 10 feet (3 m) in height.

attached the bright yellow tops to the ocean floor. The worms swayed in the ocean current like flowers in a breeze. Some were more than 6 feet (2 m) long.

Since *Alvin*'s voyage in 1977, scientists have discovered many other undersea chimneys in the Pacific, Atlantic, and Indian oceans. They have identified more than five hundred forms of life that had never been seen before.

LIFE AT THE EXTREMES

Hydrothermal vents helped scientists realize that life could exist in incredibly harsh conditions. Most forms of life on Earth's surface enjoy a world that is neither too hot nor too cold. Other conditions, such as the air or water pressure, also are mild.

However, organisms living around hydrothermal vents are built for extremely hostile conditions. They

EVER *Wonder?*

What is the hardiest form of life ever discovered at a hydrothermal vent? It is a microbe named Strain 121. Scientists discovered it in 2003 at a hydrothermal vent off the coast of Washington State. This microscopic organism can survive temperatures of 250°F (121°C). That's hotter than boiling water. Several other extreme thermophiles can live at temperatures above 176°F (80°C), which is hot enough to blister human skin on contact.

Right: *Scientists named this area near a hydrothermal vent the Rose Garden because of the red and white tubeworms that live there. Below left: These microscopic bacteria, shown in blue, survive in the high temperatures created by hydrothermal vents. Below right: Pink jellyfish flock near the Medusa hydrothermal vent field, near Costa Rica.*

are called extremophiles. (*Phile* means "lover of.") These forms of life, which are mainly microscopic bacteria, grow best under conditions that would not support most living things. For example, thermophiles thrive at scorching hot temperatures. Barophiles love high-pressure zones such as the deep ocean. Scientists are exploring where else extremophiles may live.

Some of these microbes are proving useful in the world above. Scientists are discovering helpful ways to use enzymes (chemicals) that the microbes make. For instance, enzymes from thermophiles are being used to make stonewashed jeans. They give the jeans that well-worn look and soft feel. They can withstand the very hot water used in the stonewash process. In the

"The landscape of the thermal vents is one of the most amazing sights on Earth."
—marine author and artist Richard Ellis, writing about the deep ocean in 1966

A New View of Life

Hydrothermal vents changed our view of where life could exist on Earth and how it survives. Scientists once believed that only worms and other small animals lived in the deep oceans. These animals do live in mud on the seafloor. They get food from plants and animals closer to the surface that died and sank to the bottom.

Hydrothermal vents showed that a huge variety of other living things thrive in the deep oceans too. But they get their energy from minerals in hydrothermal vent water instead of from sunlight.

future, microbes from these extreme environments may even help us understand whether—and how—life exists in space.

Worries about the Wonder

Hydrothermal vents are a natural part of Earth's moving plates. Plates shift around, so the locations of hydrothermal vents do too. Vents in one area can weaken or shut off. And new cracks in the seafloor allow vents to form in other places. But there are no threats to their continued existence. And wherever hydrothermal vents crop up, vent dwellers seem to find them. Scientists still don't know exactly how these creatures locate the vents.

In a 2005 study, scientists took samples of a hydrothermal vent. This slice of rock shows the chimney holes through which minerals passed. It also shows rings of different kinds of minerals that passed through the vent over time.

4 THE GREAT Barrier Reef

Parts of the Great Barrier Reef rise above the ocean's surface. But most of the reef lies beneath the water.

*C*APTAIN JAMES COOK AND THE CREW

OF THE HMB *ENDEAVOUR* WERE EXPLORING AUSTRALIA'S EASTERN

COAST IN 1770. NO EUROPEAN HAD EVER SEEN THIS PART OF THE

WORLD. NEAR MIDNIGHT ON JUNE 11, THE *ENDEAVOUR* SAILED SILENTLY

THROUGH THE SEA. SUDDENLY THE SHIP CRASHED INTO SOMETHING

JUST BENEATH THE WATER. AGAIN AND AGAIN, THE SHIP WAS LIFTED AND

THROWN ONTO THE ROCKY ROADBLOCK BELOW. SOON IT WAS STUCK.

Endeavour had landed on a reef, a rocky ocean ridge that nearly reaches the surface. The crew threw cannons, crates of food, and barrels of water overboard to lighten the ship. Then it would float higher in the water. But the *Endeavour* was not able to float off the reef until the next night.

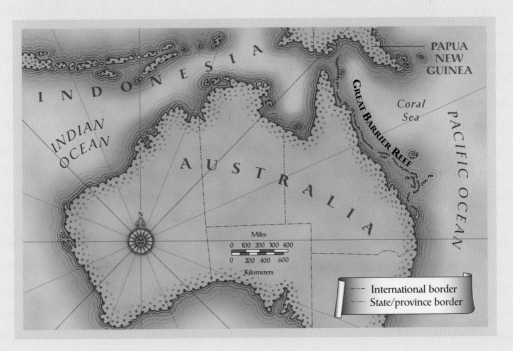

Captain Cook's ship, the HMB Endeavour, lies beached on the Great Barrier Reef. Sydney Parkinson, the artist assigned to the expedition, drew this picture in 1770. It is the first known picture of Australia created by a non-Australian.

Cook did not know it, but he had just discovered the Great Barrier Reef. It is the world's largest coral reef. The reef is vast, stretching for more than 1,430 miles (2,300 km) from north to south. In some places, it is almost 90 miles (145 km) wide. The Great Barrier Reef covers 135,000 square miles (350,000 sq. km), an area about as large as the state of Oregon.

In fact, the Great Barrier Reef is not a single reef. It is a collection of about three thousand smaller reefs and nine hundred islands. The reefs form a barrier that blocks and protects Australia's coast from the crashing waves of the Coral Sea.

"All the dangers we had escaped were little in comparison of being thrown upon this Reef where the ship must be dashed to pieces in a moment. A reef such as is here spoke of is scarcely known in Europe. It is a wall of coral rock, rising . . . out of the unfathomable ocean."

—Captain James Cook, the first European to discover the Great Barrier Reef (in 1770)

EVER *Wonder?*

What do corals eat? Corals have tentacles with stingers. They use them to catch microscopic animals floating in the sea. But most of their food comes from tiny algae— plantlike organisms—that live inside coral. Corals and algae have a partnership, or a symbiotic relationship. Corals give algae a home. Algae give corals food. Algae release nutrients that provide coral with about 90 percent of their food.

IT'S ALIVE!

Some reefs are made from rock or sand. Coral reefs are different. They are alive. Trillions of tiny animals called coral polyps build them. Some of these soft, tube-shaped creatures are as small as the head of a pin. Others are as large as a person's hand. As certain types of polyps grow, they take bits of calcium from the seawater. They combine it with carbon dioxide in their bodies. It forms calcium carbonate. This is the same material that makes up the rock limestone.

Several types of coral grow together on this section of the Great Barrier Reef. As groups of coral polyps grow, they form a unique shape. Some look like tree branches. Others grow in the shape of a ball or a bunch of feathers. A starfish lies on top of the coral shown below.

The polyps then build a shell, called a skeleton, of calcium carbonate around their bodies. The skeletons of many polyps are joined together on a reef. Polyps keep building up taller skeletons over time. When polyps die, they leave those hard skeletons behind. Over the years, hundreds of trillions of coral skeletons make a coral reef larger and larger. The Great Barrier Reef is the largest structure on Earth made by living creatures.

Below: *Schools of fish swim around a section of the Great Barrier Reef.* **Inset:** *These turret corals look like yellow flowers when open. They use their many tentacles to pull food out of the water.*

Left: *A blue sea star crosses a field of coral on the Great Barrier Reef. While the blue sea star does not eat coral, some other starfish do.* Right: *Individual polyps of purple staghorn coral cluster together on the Great Barrier Reef.*

Corals began building the Great Barrier Reef as much as five hundred thousand years ago. (That is actually young compared to other reefs!) Several times, a drop in sea level exposed the reef. The corals died without water. When sea level rose again, new corals kept building on the old reef remains.

The present-day reef probably began growing about twenty thousand years ago. Earth then was in an ice age, with thick ice sheets covering the land. As Earth warmed and the ice melted, sea level slowly rose. Water covered hills along the Australian coast. That allowed corals to grow higher and higher on the hillsides. By about six thousand to eight thousand years ago, corals on the underwater hills had formed the reefs and islands that you can see in the modern Great Barrier Reef.

EVER *Wonder?*

How did the Great Barrier Reef get that name? British explorer Matthew Flinders gave it that name after an expedition to the reef in 1802. Until then people thought that several separate reefs were along the coast of Australia. Flinders realized that the many smaller reefs were part of one great reef system.

"In among the branches of the corals, like birds among trees, floated many beautiful fish, radiant with metallic greens or crimsons, or fantastically banded with black and yellow stripes."

—J. Beete Jukes, a British scientist who studied the Great Barrier Reef from 1842–1846

Fish, clams, sponges, starfish, and many other organisms live in and around the Great Barrier Reef.

A shrimp feeds near a spotted prawn goby on the Great Barrier Reef.

RAIN FORESTS OF THE SEA

Coral reefs are sometimes called rain forests of the sea. They may seem to have nothing in common with dense rain forests in warm, humid land areas. However, both are teeming with wildlife. Coral reefs provide shelter for thousands of animals and plants. They are home to colorful fish, shellfish, starfish, sharks, dolphins, and turtles. More than two hundred kinds of birds soar above the reef or live on its beaches and islands.

Only tropical rain forests have a greater variety of living things than the Great Barrier Reef. The reef is one of Earth's most complex ecosystems. In an ecosystem, the plants and animals in a community interact with one another and their environment. One is dependent on another for survival. Some even form partnerships in which each helps the other. This is called symbiosis.

Along the Great Barrier Reef, fish called gobies form a partnership with shrimp. Some gobies share a home with shrimp that dig tunnels in the sand. The goby gets to live and lay its eggs in the tunnel. The shrimp gets a watchman. The goby has much better eyesight to spy enemies approaching. When alarmed, it flicks its tail or flees into the tunnel. The shrimp senses this movement and also swims to safety. Other reef animals form partnerships in which they help one another stay clean or find food.

Above: *A green turtle glides over the Great Barrier Reef.* Inset: *Two dwarf minke whales dive in the deep water off the Great Barrier Reef.*

The Great Barrier Reef also is a temporary home to some very large guests. Humpback whales swim up to 3,100 miles (5,000 km) from Antarctic waters to the reef each year. They spend time in the warm water to give birth and raise their young.

Parts of the reef's ecosystem are above the water. Some islands, for instance, provide nesting areas for seabirds. Almost two million egrets, ospreys, pelicans, sea eagles, and other birds lay eggs and raise their young there. Endangered green turtles and loggerhead turtles also breed in these areas. In addition, the Great Barrier Reef has huge areas of sea grass and mangroves. These trees and shrubs provide a home for many other animals and plants.

Coral *Bleaching*

Global warming is one of the biggest threats to the world's coral reefs. When ocean temperatures rise, coral become stressed and push out algae that live inside their bodies. This is called coral bleaching. Algae give corals their bold color as well as nutrients. Without their algae, the corals turn white *(below)* and soon die.

Worries about the Wonder

The government of Australia takes great care to preserve this natural wonder of the world. It has set aside a huge area around the reef as the Great Barrier Reef Marine Park. About two million people visit the Great Barrier Reef each year. Some arrive on tour boats that travel near the reef so people can sightsee or fish. Others get close-up by scuba diving in the ocean around the reef.

Visitors must obey rules that protect coral and other animals and plants. One park rule says that divers should not touch the reef. Simply handling or stepping on coral can kill it (and sometimes can hurt humans). Fishers can catch only certain numbers of fish around the reef. This ensures that enough fish are left each year to reproduce. Some areas or species are completely off-limits for fishing. Laws also control the amount of sewage and other pollution that cities along the coast can release. That pollution can kill coral.

One of the greatest dangers to the Great Barrier Reef comes from global warming. This warming is raising the temperature of the oceans everywhere. Corals can't live if the water becomes too warm. Pollution from around the world harms corals in other ways too.

Laws cannot protect the Great Barrier Reef from natural threats. Hurricanes and other storms can break off sections of a reef. The crown-of-thorns starfish causes enormous damage to the reef by eating coral. But scientists are working hard to find better ways of protecting the reef. They want to make sure that it remains a wonder in the centuries ahead.

5 Bay of Fundy

The Bay of Fundy in New Brunswick, Canada, is famous for its high ocean tides.

*I*N 1604 FRENCH EXPLORER SAMUEL

DE CHAMPLAIN DISCOVERED ONE OF EARTH'S MOST UNUSUAL

BODIES OF WATER. CHAMPLAIN HAD SAILED FROM FRANCE TO THE

ATLANTIC COAST OF CANADA. HE PLANNED TO SET UP THE FIRST

FRENCH SETTLEMENT IN NORTH AMERICA.

Champlain discovered a long, narrow ocean bay. The bay's mouth is about 50 miles (80 km) wide. Its sides form a pocket about 150 miles (241 km) long between the modern Canadian provinces of New Brunswick and Nova Scotia. Champlain called this body of water French Bay. It later became known as the Bay of Fundy.

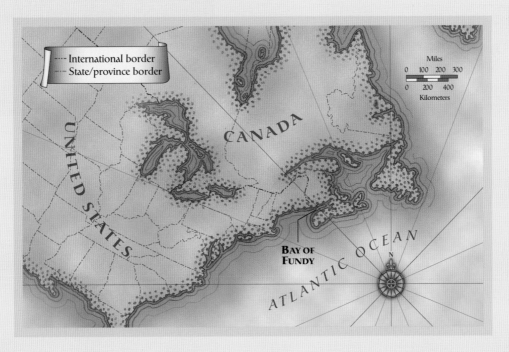

Much of the water, however, did not stay in the bay all the time. It sloshed in and out twice a day. A person could stand on dry land in the morning. By midday that land would be under water as high as a four-story building. Come evening, it would be dry once again. This occurs because the Bay of Fundy has the world's highest tides—the daily rise and fall of water along the seashore.

TITANIC TIDES

Everyone who has spent time at an ocean beach has seen tides. At low tide, water retreats out to sea. This uncovers the ocean bottom and makes the beach seem bigger. Sandpipers and gulls often peck in the wet sand for a tasty meal of worms, crabs, or fish eggs.

At high tide, the water rushes back up onto shore. It covers more of the beach again. Sometimes, high tide leaves a line of seaweed on the sand, marking the water's highest point.

The difference between high and low tides is called the tidal range. It varies from place to place. In Boston, Massachusetts, an extremely high tide

FLOWERPOT *Rocks*

Rushing water in the strong tides wears away softer rock in cliffs surrounding the bay. Harder rock, however, stays in place. In some areas, the water has carved the rock into interesting shapes. Some look like arches. Others resemble tall, skinny mushrooms. At high tide, only the top of each can be seen. It looks like a small island with trees growing on top. At low tide, the whole rock can be seen. Tourists walk under the arches on the beach. Because of the rocks' color and shape, they resemble flowerpots. They are called flowerpot rocks.

"We went out in the afternoon and looked at the tide coming up the Petitcodiac River. . . . It came rolling over the flats with immense fury, carrying stones and mud before it and making a fearful noise."

—James Brown, a school commissioner in Nova Scotia, describing the effect of the incoming tide on a river feeding into the Bay of Fundy in 1844

may be 15 feet (4.5 m) higher than low tide. In Los Angeles, California, water level during an extreme high tide may be 8 feet (2.5 m) higher than low tide. In contrast, a high tide at the most inland part of the Bay of Fundy may be 60 feet (18 m) higher than low tide. Extreme high tides can exceed 66 feet (20 m).

Twice each day, about 100 billion tons (91 billion metric tons) of seawater slosh in and out of the Bay of Fundy. The bay fills and empties in a flow of water that is greater than the daily combined flow of the world's freshwater rivers.

Top left: *This satellite photo shows the Bay of Fundy at high tide. The deepest water appears in dark purple. Bottom left: At low tide, most of the water withdraws from the bay. Dark purple stripes show low areas where water is trapped between tides.*

Above: *When the tide is in, boats in Hall's Harbor in the Bay of Fundy float at the docks.*
Below: *When the tide is out, the same boats rest on the ground.*

People traveling in boats must be careful in the Bay of Fundy. The rushing tides can strand boats on dry land or trap them by flooding passages like this one.

TUGS AND TIDES

People have lived and worked along ocean shores for thousands of years. They know that water regularly rises and falls along the shore. Sailors learned to pay attention to tides. Ships trying to enter a shallow harbor may wait for high tide to avoid running aground on the seafloor. Or ships may need a low tide to be able to pass under low bridges. Tides also create fast-rushing currents of water. These may catch boats and push them off course or make them crash onto rocks.

For centuries, people found different ways to explain why tides happen. The ancestors of the Micmac people, native Canadians who live in the Bay of Fundy area, said that a giant whale swam through the bay. It created the back-and-forth slosh with a flip of its mighty tail. The ancient Chinese thought that tides happened because Earth breathes. Water rushed onto shore when Earth inhaled, and low tides happened when the planet exhaled.

In 1687 English scientist Sir Isaac Newton discovered what really causes ocean tides. They happen mainly because of the gravitational pull of the moon. Earth's gravity pulls things toward the ground. In the same way, gravity from the moon tugs and pulls at Earth.

"In this [northeast] part of the Bay of Fundy, the tide rises extremely rapidly, and can reach a . . . height of seventy feet [21 m]."
—Henri-Raymond Casgrain, a writer who visited the bay in 1887

The bay's shape helps create high tides in another way too. It gets narrower and shallower toward the far side. All that water from the natural sloshing and tides gets squeezed into a smaller space, and it gets forced high up onto the shore.

The strong tides also affect the Saint John River and other rivers flowing into the Bay of Fundy. As high tide rushes in against the river flow, the tidewater actually reverses the flow of these rivers. Scientists call this a tidal bore. These strange backflows happen on only about sixty rivers in the world. When the flow of the Saint John River reverses at high tide, water flows backward over rocks. This forms the famous Reversing Falls in the city of Saint John, New Brunswick. Tourists are encouraged to visit the falls at low tide and again at high tide to see the water flow both ways.

WORRIES ABOUT THE WONDER

The Bay of Fundy is one of the most popular tourist areas in eastern Canada. Thousands of people visit each year to watch the tides or see

At the Reversing Falls in Saint John, New Brunswick, the force of the incoming tide is greater than that of the river's natural flow into the ocean. As the tide rises, the clash between river and ocean creates dangerous rapids. Boats can pass safely only at times when the push of river and ocean are almost equal.

A whale dives in the Bay of Fundy. Tourists come to watch the many whales that migrate through the bay. To protect the whales from being struck and killed by boats, the Canadian government has set a speed limit on boats in some parts of the bay.

whales in the bay. Many local people work in hotels, restaurants, and sightseeing boats that serve tourists.

Some locals are concerned about proposals to use the bay's tides to generate electricity. These ideas call for placing lines of floating barges in some areas of the bay. Linked together like the cars of a train, the barges would have electric generators powered by the tidal flow.

These generators would produce electricity without polluting the air. However, local people worry that they could spoil the natural beauty of the Bay of Fundy. Then fewer tourists might visit the area. Local people might lose jobs and income.

"It is known that the Bay of Fundy is famous for the rapid rise of the tide, as well as for the enormous difference between the height of low and high waters. . . . [The tidal bore] can be heard coming from very far away, making a loud noise. It is a furious torrent, rising six to ten feet [2 to 3 m] above the river, running up with a rolling motion and terrible smashing sounds."

—Joseph-Octave Plessis, bishop of Quebec, who visited the bay area in 1812

North Pole

A polar bear and her cubs travel across the packed snow and ice near the North Pole.

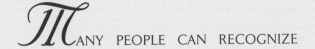ANY PEOPLE CAN RECOGNIZE

POLAR BEARS BY THEIR WHITE FUR. THESE BEARS ARE OFTEN AN

ATTRACTION AT ZOOS. VISITORS CAN WATCH THEM LUMBER AROUND

ON THEIR HUGE PAWS OR GO FOR A SWIM.

Far fewer people have seen polar bears in their natural habitat. They live in the frozen Arctic region around the North Pole. Not many people see the bears there because the North Pole is not located on solid land. It is on ice that floats on the Arctic Ocean.

The ice cover at the North Pole is called the Arctic ice cap. The ice can be up to 15 feet (4.6 m) thick. The weather at the pole is bitterly cold, snowy, and windy. This is due to the pole's location, about 450 miles (725 km) north of Greenland. The North Pole is the northernmost point on Earth. That means the pole receives less direct heat from the sun than anywhere else in the Northern Hemisphere.

On a globe, lines of latitude run parallel to the equator. Latitude measures how far north or south of the equator a place is located. The measurements use a scale of degrees from 0 to 90. The equator, which runs around the middle of Earth, has a latitude of 0 degrees. But 90 degrees north latitude marks just one spot: the North Pole. It is sometimes called true north. If you're standing at the North Pole, everything else in the world is located to your south. (A globe's longitude lines—its vertical lines—also meet at this spot.)

The North Pole is the end of Earth, or rather, one end of Earth's axis. The axis runs from the North Pole to the South Pole. This imaginary line is the center around which the planet rotates every twenty-four hours. The tilt of the axis changes the amount of sunlight that reaches different parts of Earth's surface throughout the year. Winter happens in the Northern Hemisphere when the top of the axis is tilted away from the sun. Warm weather comes in summer as the Northern Hemisphere tilts toward the sun.

A sign marks the exact point of the North Pole—at least for a few minutes. Because the Arctic is covered with water and constantly shifting plates of ice, no marker of the North Pole's location remains accurate for very long. The ice will eventually float away from the exact spot.

Above: *Sunlight hitting fog on the Arctic Ocean creates a pure white fog bow.* **Inset:** *During the Arctic summer, seals dive for fish beneath the ocean's broken ice cover.*

Areas near the equator are not affected much by the tilt. The sun shines directly on that part of Earth all year. But at the poles, the tilt has a big effect. The sun's rays hit the poles at a wide angle. The light is weaker and produces less heat to warm the surface. Snow and ice naturally build up in this frigid polar climate. The snow and ice also reflect much of the sunlight that does arrive, instead of absorbing it as heat.

A Long Day's Night

Weather at the North Pole is very cold in both winter and summer. In winter, temperatures average -30°F (-34°C). Summer weather warms up to an average of 32°F (0°C). Winter blizzards, with howling wind and deep snow, can last for several days. Snowstorms also can happen in the summer, along with rain and fog.

Weather that extreme is found in a few other places on Earth, such as high mountain peaks. But sunrises and sunsets at the North Pole are even more unusual. In most of the world, the sun rises once a day and sets once a day. At the North Pole, however, the sun rises and sets only once each year! This happens because of the way Earth is tilted on its axis as it revolves around the sun.

Water trickles off an iceberg on the coast of Greenland during the long Arctic summer days.

"Naturally, there were frequent storms and intense cold. . . . I have seen rocks a hundred and a hundred and fifty pounds [45 to 68 kg] in weight picked up by the storm and blown for distances of ninety or a hundred feet [27 to 30 m] . . . believe me, I have been afraid."

—Matthew A. Henson, African American explorer who accompanied Robert E. Peary to the North Pole in 1909

The sunrise at the North Pole lasts several days. On the spring equinox, about March 21, half the sun is above the horizon. Slowly it fully appears. It shines twenty-four hours a day until early fall. The sun finally sets around the autumn equinox, about September 21. It gradually falls below the horizon again. Some light is still visible, in constant twilight, until early October. Then the North Pole is in complete darkness for the winter. Twilight returns in early March as the spring equinox and sunrise approach.

LAND OF THE MIDNIGHT SUN

The Arctic, the large area that surrounds the North Pole, shares some of these unusual conditions. Throughout the Arctic, the summer sky is still bright late at night. The region sometimes is called the Land of the Midnight Sun for this reason. The Arctic includes parts of Alaska, Canada, Greenland, Iceland, Norway, Sweden, Finland, and Russia. The Bering, Beaufort, and Chukchi seas also are in the Arctic.

People do not live permanently at the North Pole. But some people live in other parts of the Arctic. They include native peoples, such as the Inuit and Aleut, who were the original inhabitants of Alaska.

Much of the Arctic is treeless, frozen land covered with snow or ice year-round. Farming is difficult or impossible in most areas. Native people often depend on fishing and hunting for food. The Arctic also has rich deposits of oil and other natural resources. These provide jobs and money for residents.

The sun shines through the night over Svalbard, a group of Norwegian islands in the Arctic Ocean.

REACHING FOR THE POLE

People from Europe first became interested in the Arctic in the 1500s. Explorers began searching for a water route across northern North America. This "Northwest Passage" would connect the Atlantic and the Pacific oceans. Explorers hoped that this route would be a shortcut between Europe and Asia. It would make trade easier. Famous explorers such as Henry Hudson, John Cabot, and Jacques Cartier sailed in search of the Northwest Passage.

Hope of finding the shortcut eventually faded. But soon explorers in the United States and Europe became interested in reaching the North Pole. Any explorer who set foot on the North Pole would earn widespread fame. Expeditions sailed north until sea ice blocked their ships from going farther. Then they set out over the ice in wooden sleds pulled by dog teams.

These journeys were terribly difficult. It was bitterly cold. The ice was not flat but covered with jagged mounds and cracks. The ice also moved up to 12 miles (20 km) in one night. If the expedition managed to travel 15 miles (24 km) during the day, the next morning, the explorers might discover they were only 3 miles (5 km) ahead of their starting point.

Many brave explorers failed. Some got lost in the barren landscape.

English explorer Henry Hudson visited the Arctic in the 1600s.

EVER *Wonder?*

Did anyone ever find the Northwest Passage connecting the Atlantic and Pacific oceans? For centuries, explorers looked for a faster route to China. They searched for a passageway through the ice-covered Arctic Ocean. That ice prevented ships from sailing through the area. In 1903 Norwegian explorer Roald Amundsen led the first expedition to sail successfully between the two oceans. For more than two years, he looked for places where the ice had briefly melted enough to sail through. Global warming may eventually keep the area ice-free year-round. The passage could open to regular shipping.

"The Northwest Passage—that baffling mystery to all the navigators of the past—was at last to be ours. . . . We had succeeded. . . . Victory was ours!"

—Roald Amundsen, describing his feelings after discovering the Northwest Passage in 1905

Others ran out of food, got sick, or suffered frostbite. They either died or had to turn back.

U.S. Navy engineer Robert Edwin Peary often gets credit for being the first person to reach the North Pole. Peary claimed to have reached the pole on April 6, 1909. African American explorer Matthew Henson and four Inuit men traveled with him. But whether Peary reached the actual pole has been questioned. Some historians say there is not enough scientific data from his journey to decide.

Other explorers have reached the North Pole since then. Airplanes have flown over the pole and landed there. Military submarines from the United States and Russia have traveled through the ocean under the North Pole. Submarines also have surfaced at the North Pole, crashing through several feet of ice cover on the Arctic Ocean.

Robert Peary photographed his team of explorers at the North Pole in 1909. Matthew Henson stands in the center with the official flag of the expedition.

Russian researchers prepare to launch a deep-diving miniature submarine toward the bottom of the Arctic Ocean in 2007.

In 2007 a Russian expedition sent the first people to the ocean bottom at the North Pole. They traveled in a submersible down to 14,114 feet (4,302 m). With the vehicle's robot arm, they planted a Russian flag in the seafloor.

THE NORTH ~~POLE~~ POLES

When people talk about the North Pole, they usually mean the geographic North Pole. However, Earth also has a north magnetic pole, which is hundreds of miles away. The magnetic pole exists because Earth has a magnetic field. It is almost like the field of a bar magnet that you might buy in a hardware store. Magnetic force flows out from one end, or pole. It flows in the other end, making a loop. Earth's magnetic poles act as the ends of the magnet.

People once thought that both the geographic and magnetic poles were in the same place. But as explorers used compasses to navigate through northern waters, they saw something odd. The magnetized needle in these instruments pointed in a direction that was not exactly true north. Rather, the needle of a compass in the Northern Hemisphere always points toward the north magnetic pole. By the 1800s, navigators

FLIGHT OVER THE
North Pole

Thousands of ordinary people fly over the North Pole area every year. Most fly in commercial airplanes going between North America and Asia. The planes fly great circle routes. Those are the shortest distance between two points on Earth. When drawn on a flat map, great circle routes do not look short. However, because of Earth's round shape, these curved flight paths can be several hours shorter than other routes.

The northern lights appear as ribbons of light over snowy hills in Arctic Finland.

realized that this magnetic pole actually is located in northern Canada.

The magnetic pole moves a little from day to day. It can move as much as 25 miles (40 km) from year to year. The movement happens because of changes in Earth's magnetic field, which scientists do not fully understand. As that movement continues, the north magnetic pole may eventually shift to Siberia in Russia.

Wherever the north magnetic pole moves, its magnetism interacts with the atmosphere. That produces the northern lights, or aurora borealis. These glowing, shimmering sheets of colored light in the sky often can be seen on clear nights.

WORRIES ABOUT THE WONDER

The North Pole and the rest of the Arctic have been under close watch in recent years because of global warming. As Earth's climate gets warmer, scientists are concerned that the polar ice cap will melt completely. That would endanger polar bears, who hunt mainly from floating ice. It would also warm the Arctic Ocean water, affecting marine life. Some scientists think the Arctic Ocean will be free of ice during the summers by 2030.

The North Pole may become warmer. But however it changes, the Land of the Midnight Sun will remain a wondrous place.

7 South Pole

Strong winds drive snow across a rocky section of Antarctica.

$\mathcal{I}$N 2004 NASA SCIENTISTS CREATED THE TUMBLEWEED ROVER. THIS ROUND ROBOT EXPLORER WAS DESIGNED TO ROLL OVER THE SURFACE OF MARS AND OTHER PLANETS. AS THE VEHICLE TRAVELED, INSTRUMENTS INSIDE WOULD SEARCH FOR TRACES OF WATER.

Before launching the rover, scientists had to make sure that it would work in the extreme conditions on Mars. They needed to test it somewhere on Earth that resembled Mars's hostile environment. NASA chose the South Pole, on the continent of Antarctica. Pushed along by the wind, the tumbleweed rover completed a 44-mile (70 km) voyage across Antarctica.

This frozen land at the bottom of Earth has been the testing ground for other spacecraft also. Antarctica's harsh environment mimics the conditions of space better than any other part of Earth.

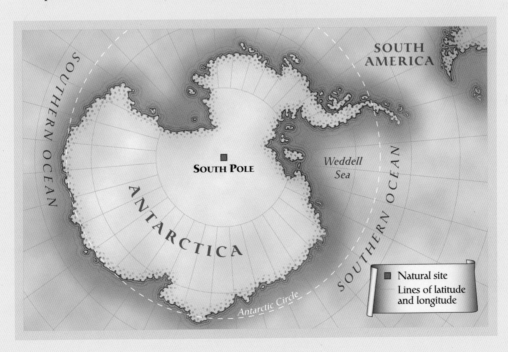

SOUTHERN OCEAN

SOUTH AMERICA

SOUTH POLE

Weddell Sea

ANTARCTICA

SOUTHERN OCEAN

Antarctic Circle

■ Natural site
— Lines of latitude and longitude

Antarctica lies in the middle of the Southern Ocean. It is the fifth-largest continent after Asia, Africa, North America, and South America. Antarctica is about the size of the United States and Mexico combined. Most of it is inside the Antarctic Circle. This imaginary boundary line marks the region around the South Pole.

BOTTOM OF THE WORLD

The geographic South Pole is located near the center of Antarctica. The South Pole is the southernmost point on Earth. It sits at 90° south latitude. A person standing at the South Pole

Below: *Icebergs and floating chunks of ice pack the Weddell Sea off Antarctica's eastern coast.* **Inset:** *Snow drifts over rocks on a barren plain in Antarctica.*

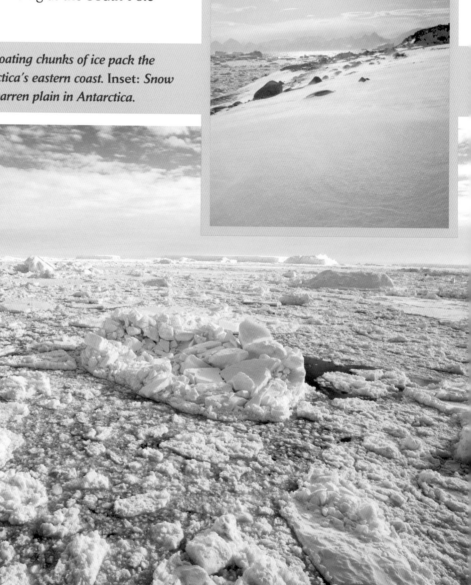

WALK AROUND THE WORLD—
in Five Seconds

People can walk all the way around the world at the South Pole. Scientists place a marker post directly over the South Pole each year. (Since the ice sheets slowly drift across the continent, the marker moves about 20 to 30 feet (7 to 10 m) per year and needs to be replaced.) The 2008 marker appears below. To travel around the world, a person must cross 360 degrees of longitude. At the equator, that would mean a journey of 25,000 miles (40,000 km). At the South Pole, it is just a few steps around the marker post.

can walk in only one direction—north. Like the north magnetic pole, the south magnetic pole is separate from the geographic pole. It is off the coast of Antarctica, toward Australia. It moves with changes in Earth's magnetic field.

Antarctica's location makes it the most remote place on Earth. It is also the world's coldest, driest, windiest place. Antarctica is colder than the Arctic because much of Antarctica is about 1.9 miles (3 km) above sea level. Temperatures are colder at these higher altitudes. In addition, the north polar area is covered by the Arctic Ocean, which stores heat from the sun and warms the area. Antarctica is mostly land covered by ice. It has no warming effect from water.

A FROZEN WORLD

On really cold winter days at the South Pole, the temperature may drop to −100°F (−73°C). On warm summer afternoons, the temperature often soars to −18°F (−28°C). At that temperature, spit freezes solid into ice before it hits the ground. But no one has ever seen the ground in most of Antarctica. Ice averaging 1 mile (1.6 km) thick covers about 98 percent of Antarctica's surface.

The sun sets over Antarctica.

The South Pole has one sunrise each year in September and one sunset in March. These happen over several days, as at the North Pole. Sunrise is the start of about six months of summer, when the sun shines twenty-four hours a day. Sunset begins a short period of twilight and then about six months of winter darkness. Terrible winter blizzards last for days, and winds exceed 100 miles (160 km) per hour.

Blizzards result mainly from the wind blowing snow already on the ground. Antarctica gets so little precipitation (rain or snow) that it is Earth's driest desert. Barely 2 inches (5 cm) of new snow fall at the South Pole each year. But this snow never melts. Instead, it piles up and turns into ice. At the South Pole, the ice has piled up almost 2 miles (3.2 km) thick.

Due to the harsh climate, no native animals or plants live at the South Pole. Animals and plants do live elsewhere in Antarctica. They must be able to survive in the extreme cold. Some plants and plantlike growth, such as mosses, lichens, and algae, survive by living inside ice and rocks.

"Thus ended July. It ended in cold, as it had been born in cold. I have the meteorological records before me now. Twenty days were 60° below [−51°C] or colder. On six days the temperature crossed −70° [−57°C]."

—*Richard E. Byrd, an American who spent five months alone in a weather station in Antarctica during the winter in 1934*

Seven Wonders of the Arctic, Antarctica, and the Oceans

Emperor penguins dive into the water to hunt beneath the Antarctic ice. They eat fish, squid, and other underwater creatures that live in these deep, cold waters. Emperor penguins live only in Antarctica.

The only human residents are about four thousand scientists who work at international research stations. Most visit during warmer weather, which begins in October in the Southern Hemisphere. They return home by February as winter approaches. Once winter sets in, travel in and out of Antarctica is impossible. Only a handful stay in winter.

EVER *Wonder?*

What animals live on this frozen continent? No animals are permanent residents of the South Pole or the area around the pole. However, birds, penguins, seals, whales, leopard seals, and fish thrive in other parts of Antarctica. Many of them live on the Antarctic Peninsula. Also known as the Palmer Peninsula, it is warmer than the rest of the continent.

A PLACE FOR ADVENTURE

Long before the first explorers visited Antarctica, people believed that Earth had a southern land. A famous ancient Greek geographer named Claudius Ptolemy was one of the earliest to predict its existence. He lived almost two thousand years ago. Ptolemy envisioned Antarctica as a lush, warm place where rich people lived in a great empire.

In the 1500s and 1600s, explorers from Spain and Portugal searched for Antarctica, then known as Terra Australis (Southern Land). Legends said that Antarctica was a tropical paradise with gold nuggets scattered on the ground like stones. In the 1800s, some people thought there was an entrance to the interior of Earth at the South Pole.

The existence of this southern land was finally confirmed once fishing ships and explorers reached Antarctica. A Russian expedition led by Fabian Gottlieb von Bellingshausen made the first confirmed sighting of the continent in 1820. Soon explorers realized how severe Antarctica's environment and the Antarctic waters were. Only a few other expeditions ventured there for the rest of the century.

In the early 1900s, explorers took on the Antarctic challenge. They competed to be the first to cross great expanses of ice to reach the South Pole. Norwegian Roald Amundsen and his team were the first to reach the pole, on December 14, 1911. British explorer Robert Falcon Scott's team reached it a month later. On the return trip, however, Scott and his four companions froze to death.

One of the greatest Antarctic adventures took place between 1914 and 1916. An expedition led by British explorer Ernest Shackleton planned to cross Antarctica. The explorers would cross the South

Above: *Norwegian explorer Roald Amundsen learned cold-weather survival skills for the South Pole on his earlier expedition to the Arctic.* Left: *Robert Falcon Scott's team stands at Amundsen's abandoned South Pole campsite.*

> *"Great God! This is an awful place and terrible. . . .*
> *Now for the run home and a desperate struggle.*
> *I wonder if we can do it?"*
> —*Robert Falcon Scott, writing in his diary in 1912, before he and his team froze to*
> *death while trying to return home from the South Pole*

This photo from Ernest Shackleton's 1914–1916 expedition shows the Endurance *trapped in ice in the Antarctic.*

Pole on dog-pulled sleds. But when they were just one day's sail from the continent, their ship, the *Endurance*, became frozen in sea ice.

They waited through the winter on board. Nearly a year later, the crew abandoned ship before the ice crushed and sank the *Endurance*. They walked over ice and sailed more than 800 miles (1,287 km) in frigid water in open boats. They finally were rescued ten months after leaving their ship. All twenty-eight men survived.

A PLACE FOR SCIENCE

In the 1950s and 1960s, the United States and other countries became interested in Antarctica for scientific research. They began building research stations there. Some scientists study distant parts of the universe at the South Pole. The dry air and high altitude give telescopes the best views of space.

Other scientists are studying how global warming might affect Antarctica's vast covering of ice. Almost 70 percent of all the freshwater on Earth is locked up in that ice. Thick sheets of ice move across the continent's surface. Some extend over water along the coastline, where chunks frequently break off and fall into the ocean. Scientists figure that if all Antarctica's ice melted, sea levels would rise about 200 feet (61 m). Many coastal cities around the world would be underwater.

Scientists also drill deep down into Antarctica's ice sheet to study how Earth's atmosphere has changed over time. In some places, deep ice formed from snowfalls five hundred thousand to one million years ago. The snow trapped air as it froze. These ice samples are called ice cores. By studying them, scientists can tell what Earth's climate was like in the distant past.

Other environmental research on Antarctica has already had global effects.

METEORITES from Mars

Antarctica is the best place for scientists to collect meteorites. Meteorites are chunks of rock or metal from space that hit Earth's surface. When meteorites land in Antarctica, they get buried inside ice sheets. Even when buried for millions of years, meteorites stay in exactly the same condition as when they first fell. Movements of the ice sheets eventually force meteorites to the surface. Scientists collect and study those space rocks. In the 1990s, scientists found an Antarctic meteorite from Mars. They studied it and found microscopic fossils of bacteria in it. Bacteria would indicate that life may have existed on Mars billions of years ago.

An Australian researcher examines an ice core removed from a glacier in Antarctica. The oldest section of this piece of ice dates to 1840.

Tourists view an enormous iceberg in Antarctica.

Scientists know that ozone gas in Earth's atmosphere filters out harmful rays from the sun. In the 1980s, they found that the protective layer of ozone above Antarctica had become thin. Certain chemicals were destroying it. Discovery of the ozone hole led countries around the world to ban those chemicals to keep from further damaging the ozone layer.

WORRIES ABOUT THE WONDER

Antarctica is not owned by any country. In the 1960s, many of the world's countries signed a treaty. They agreed to preserve and protect Antarctica as a continent for research and other peaceful uses. Scientists and other visitors follow strict rules not to harm the environment.

Antarctica's remote location limits the number of visitors. Human effects on the natural environment are not a concern. Tourism has increased in recent years, but it consists mainly of cruise ships that go to the warmer Palmer Peninsula area.

Global warming may be the biggest threat to Antarctica. Scientists know that temperatures already have gone up in the Palmer Peninsula. That area has less ice and snow. Scientists are not sure how global warming may affect the rest of Antarctica. Some worry that ice sheets along the coast will melt and disappear. But most scientists think the interior of Antarctica—especially the South Pole—will stay very, very cold.

TIMELINE

1604 French explorer Samuel de Champlain discovers the Bay of Fundy, in modern Canada.

1762 Benjamin Franklin names a mighty ocean current the Gulf Stream.

1770 James Cook discovers the Great Barrier Reef, the world's largest coral reef.

1820 Fabian Gottlieb von Bellingshausen makes the first confirmed sighting of Antarctica in ships that sailed near the continent in 1820.

1875 The British ship HMS *Challenger* discovers the Mariana Trench.

1903 Norwegian explorer Roald Amundsen leads the first expedition to successfully sail on the Northwest Passage.

1909 Robert Edwin Peary claims to reach the North Pole, accompanied by American Matthew Henson and four Inuit men.

1911 The first humans to reach the geographic South Pole are Norwegian Roald Amundsen and his party on December 14, 1911.

1951 Using echo sounding, *Challenger II* maps the entire Mariana Trench.

1960 Jacques Piccard and U.S. Navy lieutenant Don Walsh ride the *Trieste,* a submersible vehicle, to the deepest point in the ocean in the Mariana Trench.

1977 The submersible *Alvin* discovers the first hydrothermal vent.

1980s Scientists in Antarctica discover the thinning of the ozone hole and warn that further damage could cause an environmental disaster.

2003 A microbe known as Strain 121 is discovered by scientists at a hydrothermal vent off the coast of Washington State.

2007 A Russian expedition makes the first manned descent to the ocean bottom at the North Pole in a submersible vehicle.

2008 Parts of the Wilkins Ice Shelf, stretching out into the sea from the Palmer Peninsula in Antarctica, crumble as the peninsula continues to warm.

CHOOSE AN EIGHTH WONDER

Now that you've read about the seven natural wonders of the Arctic, Antarctica, and the oceans, do a little research to choose an eighth wonder. You may enjoy working with a friend.

To do your research, look at some of the websites and books listed on pages 76 and 77. Look for other places in these regions that
- *are especially large*
- *are exceptionally beautiful*
- *were unknown to foreigners for many centuries*
- *are unlike any other place on Earth*

You might even try gathering photos and writing your own chapter on the eighth wonder!

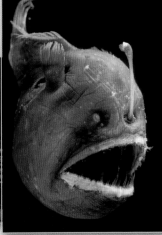

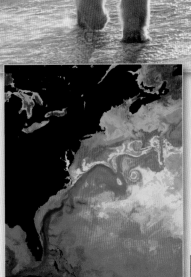

GLOSSARY AND PRONUNCIATION GUIDE

centrifugal (sen-TRIHF-yoo-guhl) force: a force that causes parts of something that is rotating to move outward from the rotating thing. This force causes high tides on the side of Earth facing away from the moon.

coral polyps: small sea animals related to jellyfish. Some kinds of corals build reefs.

current: a flow of swiftly moving water that follows a path. Ocean currents carry water from one part of an ocean to another.

global warming: an increase in Earth's average temperature due to increased carbon dioxide and other gases in the atmosphere

hydrothermal vents: openings in the ocean floor that release hot, mineral-rich water. These vents support rare forms of life at the bottom of the ocean.

reef: an ocean ridge of coral, rock, or sand

submersible (sub-MUR-sih-bul): a small submarine that can take one or more people deep underwater for scientific research

tides: the regular rise and fall of sea level along coasts, caused mainly by gravitational forces from the moon and sun

trench: a long, narrow ditch. An ocean trench is a deep valley in the ocean floor formed where one plate of rock in Earth's surface plunges under another.

SOURCE NOTES

10 PBS, "The American Experience/Alone on the Ice/William Beebe: Going Deeper," *PBS Online*, 1999, http://www.pbs.org/wgbh/amex/ice/sfeature/beebe.html (September 16, 2008).

12 BJSOnline, "Seven Miles Down: The Story of the Bathyscaph *Trieste*," *BJSonline.com*, January 2006, http://bjsonline.com/watches/articles/0022_3.shtml (September 16, 2008).

14 Jack Williams, "Dr. Andreas Rechnitzer, 80; Deep-Sea Exploration Pioneer," *San Diego Union-Tribune*, August 25, 2005, http://www.signonsandiego.com/uniontrib/20050825/news_1m25rechnitz.html (September 16, 2008).

18 Ferdinand C. Lane, *The Mysterious Sea* (Garden City, NY: Doubleday & Co., 1947), 43.

19 Benjamin Franklin, unpublished letter to Julien-David LeRoy, February 1784, *Benjamin Franklin Papers*, 2007, http://www.franklinpapers.org (September 16, 2008).

21 Thomas Yocum, "The Gulf Stream: A River in the Ocean," *CoastalGuide*, 2007, http://coastalguide.com/bearings/gulfstream.shtml (September 16, 2008).

26 National Research Council, *50 Years of Ocean Discovery: National Science Foundation 1950–2000* (Washington, DC: National Academy Press, 2000), 76.

28 Robert Ballard, *The Eternal Darkness: A Personal History of Deep-Sea Exploration* (Princeton, NJ: Princeton University Press, 2000), 176.

30 Richard Ellis, *Deep Atlantic: Life, Death, and Exploration in the Abyss* (New York: Alfred A. Knopf, 1996), 111.

34 Nicholas Thomas, *Cook: The Extraordinary Voyages of Captain James Cook* (New York: Walker & Company, 2003), 126.

38 Australian Institute of Marine Science, "Coral Reefs and Climate Change 2007," February 2007, *Australian Institute of Marine Science*, http://www3.aims.gov.au/pages/about/communications/issues/coral-reefs-and-climate-change-2007.html (September 16, 2008).

44 Petitcodiac Riverkeeper, "Petitcodiac—250 Years of Anecdotes," *Sentinelles Petitcodiac Riverkeeper*, February 2001, http://www.petitcodiac.org/riverkeeper/Documents/Bore3.doc (September 16, 2008).

47 Ibid.

51 Ibid.

56 Matthew A. Henson, *A Negro Explorer at the North Pole* (New York: Frederick A. Stokes, 1912), 21.

59 Roald Amundsen, "NOVA: Arctic Passage: My Life as an Explorer," *PBS*, February 2006, http://pbs.org/wgbh/nova/arctic/amundsen.html (September 18, 2007).

66 Richard E. Byrd, *Alone* (New York: G. P. Putnam's Sons, 1938), 270.

69 Robert Falcon Scott, *Scott's Last Expedition* (London: Smith, Elder & Co., 1913), 396.

SELECTED BIBLIOGRAPHY

American Museum of Natural History. *Ocean.* New York: Dorling Kindersley, 2006.

Ballard, Robert. *The Eternal Darkness: A Personal History of Deep-Sea Exploration.* Princeton, NJ: Princeton University Press, 2000.

Day, Trevor. *Biomes of the Earth: Oceans.* New York: Chelsea House, 2006.

Ellis, Richard. *Deep Atlantic: Life, Death, and Exploration in the Abyss.* New York: Alfred A. Knopf, 1996.

Hancock, Paul, and Brian J. Skinner, eds. *The Oxford Companion to the Earth.* Oxford: Oxford University Press, 2000.

Holliday, Les. *Coral Reefs.* Morris Plains, NJ: Salamander Books, 1989.

Leppman, Elizabeth J. *Australia and the Pacific.* Philadelphia: Chelsea House, 2006.

Luhr, James F., ed. *Earth.* London: Dorling Kindersley, 2003.

Ocean Studies Board, National Research Council. *50 Years of Ocean Discovery: National Science Foundation 1950–2000.* Washington, DC: National Academy Press, 2000.

Prager, Ellen J. *The Oceans.* New York: McGraw-Hill, 2000.

Rozwadowski, Helen M. *Fathoming the Ocean: The Discovery and Exploration of the Deep Sea.* Cambridge, MA: Belknap Press of Harvard University Press, 2005.

Shackleton, Ernest. *The Heart of the Antarctic: The Farthest South Expedition, 1907–1909.* New York: New American Library, 2000.

Thomas, Nicholas. *Cook: The Extraordinary Voyages of Captain James Cook.* New York: Walker & Company, 2003.

Thurman, Harold V. *Essentials of Oceanography.* Saddle River, NJ: Prentice Hall, 2002.

FURTHER READING AND WEBSITES

Books

Allaby, Michael. *Biomes of the World: Oceans.* Canbury, CT: Grolier Educational, 1999. Learn about the animals of the oceans as well as islands, coral reefs, and the problems with overfishing and pollution.

Baker, Beth. *Sylvia Earle.* Minneapolis: Twenty-first Century Books, 2001. At a time when women didn't usually work in science, Sylvia Earle became a marine biologist and one of the foremost defenders of the sea and its creatures.

Byrd, Richard E. *Alone.* New York: G. P. Putnam's Sons, 1938. This is Byrd's account of his struggles to stay alive, alone, at his base in Antarctica.

Hall, Michele, and Howard Hall. *Secrets of the Ocean Realm.* New York: Carroll & Graf Publishers, 1997. Check out the authors' incredible photographs of ocean life and their stories of how they took the photos, which include swimming with hammerhead sharks.

Heacox, Kim. *Antarctica: The Last Continent.* Washington, DC: National Geographic Society, 1998. Gorgeous photographs show the diversity of life on Antarctica. This book includes plenty of information about the early explorers and their courageous journeys.

Hesse, Karen. *Stowaway.* New York: Margaret K. McElderry Books, 2000. In this fictional story, Nicholas Young stows away on James Cook's ship, the HMB *Endeavor*, as it embarks on a mysterious mission. Find out what happens—through Nicholas's eyes—when the ship gets stuck on the Great Barrier Reef.

Johnson, Rebecca L. *Ernest Shackleton: Gripped by the Antarctic.* Minneapolis: Twenty-First Century Books, 2003. When Ernest Shackleton's ship, the *Endurance*, became icebound in Antarctica, Shackleton and his crew survived nineteen months before being rescued.

Mallory, Kenneth. *Diving to a Deep-Sea Volcano.* Boston: Houghton Mifflin Company, 2006. Join marine biologist Rich Lutz on his research submarine as he investigates an underwater habitat that was almost destroyed by a volcanic eruption.

Verne, Jules. *Twenty Thousand Leagues under the Sea.* London: Sampson Low, Marston, Low and Searle, 1873. In this classic tale, join Captain Nemo on his submarine, *Nautilus*, as he explores underwater wonders and tracks down sea monsters that are sinking ships.

Websites

Cool Antarctica
http://www.coolantarctica.com/
Check out photos of actual icebergs and glaciers, follow the adventures of explorers, and watch a slide show starring Adélie penguins!

Explore the Mariana Trench
http://www.marianatrench.com/
Learn how oceanographers explore the seafloor around the Mariana Trench, the deepest part of the ocean.

The Phenomenal Bay of Fundy
http://bayoffundytourism.com/
Discover the world's highest tides, and see photos of the bay's incredible landscape at high and low tide.

The Reef Education Network University of Queensland, Australia
http://www.reef.edu.au/
Surf this site and discover how corals form reefs, see creatures who live on reefs, and learn about efforts to preserve the reefs from damage.

Welcome to Tides and Water Levels
http://oceanservice.noaa.gov/education/kits/tides/welcome.html
This site is packed full of information about tides and how they affect oceans and shores. It offers user-friendly explanations and answers common questions about tides.

INDEX

ABOUT THE AUTHORS

Michael Woods is a science and medical journalist in Washington, D.C. He has won many national writing awards. Mary B. Woods is a school librarian. Their past books include the eight-volume Ancient Technology series, the fifteen-volume Disasters Up Close series, and the seven-volume Ancient Wonders of the World books. The Woodses have four children. When not writing, reading, or enjoying their grandchildren, the Woodses travel to gather material for future books.

PHOTO ACKNOWLEDGMENTS

The images in this book are used with the permission of: © Fred Bavendam/Minden Pictures, p. 5; © Planetary Visions Ltd./Photo Researchers, Inc., p. 6; © Laura Westlund/Independent Picture Service, pp. 7, 17, 25, 33, 43, 53, 63; © Matthieu Ricard/The Image Bank/Getty Images, p. 8 (top); NOAA Office of Ocean Exploration, Pacific Ring of Fire 2004 Expedition, Dr. Bob Embley, pp. 8 (inset), 14; © JAMSTEC, pp. 9, 13 (top, bottom right); © Norbert Wu/Minden Pictures, pp. 10 (both), 36 (bottom); © Donna C. Rona/Bruce Coleman/Photoshot, p. 11 (top); © Mansell/Time & Life Pictures/Getty Images, p. 11 (bottom); NOAA National Ocean Service, Steve Nicklas, p. 12; NOAA, pp. 13 (bottom left), 19, 73 (bottom left); NOAA Pacific Islands Fisheries Science Center, Coral Reef Ecosystem Division, A.Palmer, p. 15; © Cameron Davidson/Photographer's Choice/Getty Images, p. 16; NASA, pp. 18, 21, 45 (both), 73 (bottom right); © Gavin Hellier/Robert Harding World Imagery/Getty Images, p. 20; © Grant Faint/Photographer's Choice/Getty Images, p. 22; © B. Murton/Southampton Oceanography Centre/Photo Researchers, Inc., p. 24; © Emory Kristof and Alvin Chandler/National Geographic Image Collection, p. 26 (top); Photo by Robert D. Ballard, Woods Hole Oceanographic Institution, p. 26 (bottom); Photo by Dudley Foster, Woods Hole Oceanographic Institution, p. 27; University of Washington, p. 28; NOAA National Undersea Research Program, College of William & Mary, p. 29; Photo by Dr. Kathleen Crane, Woods Hole Oceanographic Institution, p. 30 (top); © Mona Lisa Production/Photo Researchers, Inc., p. 30 (bottom left); Photo by Woods Hole Oceanographic Institution, p. 30 (bottom right); NOAA Galápagos 2005 Expedition, UCSB, Univ. S. Carolina, WHOI, p. 31; © age fotostock/SuperStock, pp. 32, 37 (left); © The British Library/HIP/The Image Works, p. 34; © Robin Smith/Art Directors & TRIP, p. 35; © L. Newman & A. Flowers/Photo Researchers, Inc., p. 36 (inset); NOAA National Ocean Service, Dr. Robert Ricker, p. 37 (right); © Margo Steley/Alamy, p. 38; © Danita Delimont/Alamy, p. 39; © Jeff Hunter/Photographer's Choice/Getty Images, p. 40 (top); © Kevin Schafer/Alamy, p. 40 (inset); NOAA Coral Kingdom Collection, David Burdick, p. 41; © Darwin Wiggett/All Canada Photos/Getty Images, p. 42; © Everett C Johnson-Stock Connection/Science Faction/Getty Images, p. 46 (both); © Steve Bly/Alamy, p. 47; © Dick Keen/Visuals Unlimited, Inc., p. 48 (both); © Georg Gerster/Photo Researchers, Inc., p. 49; © All Canada Photos/Alamy, p. 50; © Gary Neil Corbett/SuperStock, p. 51; © Sue Flood/The Image Bank/Getty Images, p. 52; © Bryan & Cherry Alexander Photography/Alamy, p. 54; © Sue Flood/Stone/Getty Images, p. 55 (top); © Ralph Lee Hopkins/National Geographic/Getty Images, pp. 55 (inset), 57; © Paul Souders/The Image Bank/Getty Images, p. 56; © Stock Montage/Hulton Archive/Getty Images, p. 58; National Archives, p. 59; AP Photo/Vladimir Chistyakov, p. 60; © Norman Price/Art Directors & TRIP, p. 61; © Robert Harding/Digital Vision/Getty Images, p. 62; © Thorsten Milse/Robert Harding World Imagery/Getty Images, p. 64 (bottom); © Geoff Renner/Robert Harding World Imagery/Getty Images, p. 64 (inset); © Glenn Grant/National Science Foundation, p. 65; © Daisy Gilardini/The Image Bank/Getty Images, p. 66; © Royalty-Free/CORBIS, p. 67; © Mary Evans Picture Library/Alamy, p. 68 (left); The Illustrated London News, p. 68 (right); © Popperfoto/Getty Images, p. 69; © Vin Morgan/AFP/Getty Images, p. 70; © Colin Monteath/Minden Pictures, p. 71; © Norbert Wu/Minden Pictures/Getty Images, p. 73 (top left, top right); © James P. Blair/National Geographic/Getty Images, p. 73 (top center); © David E. Meyers/Riser/Getty Images, p. 73 (center right); © Gary Bell/Taxi/Getty Images, p. 73 (bottom center).

Front Cover: © Norbert Wu/Minden Pictures/Getty Images (top left, bottom left); © James P. Blair/National Geographic/Getty Images (top center); © David E. Meyers/Riser/Getty Images (top right); © Gary Bell/Taxi/Getty Images (center); NASA (bottom center); NOAA (bottom right).